PROVERBS FOR A GREAT LEADER

Lorenzo Jesus Serrano

Trilogy Christian Publishers
A Wholly Owned Subsidiary of Trinity Broadcasting Network
2442 Michelle Drive
Tustin, CA 92780
Copyright © 2024 by Lorenzo Serrano

Scripture quotations marked NKJV are taken from the New King James Version®. Copyright © 1982 by Thomas Nelson. Used by permission. All rights reserved. Scripture quotations marked ESV are taken from the ESV® Bible (The Holy Bible, English Standard Version®), copyright © 2001 by Crossway Bibles, a publishing ministry of Good News Publishers. Used by permission. All rights reserved. Scripture quotations marked NIV are taken from the Holy Bible, New International Version®, NIV®. Copyright © 1973, 1978, 1984, 2011 by Biblica, Inc.TM Used by permission of Zondervan. All rights reserved worldwide. www.zondervan.com. The "NIV" and "New International Version" are trademarks registered in the United States Patent and Trademark Office by Biblica, Inc.TM

All rights reserved, including the right to reproduce this book or portions thereof in any form whatsoever. For information, address Trilogy Christian Publishing Rights Department, 2442 Michelle Drive, Tustin, CA 92780. Trilogy Christian Publishing/ TBN and colophon are trademarks of Trinity Broadcasting Network.
For information about special discounts for bulk purchases, please contact Trilogy Christian Publishing.

Trilogy Disclaimer: The views and content expressed in this book are those of the author and may not necessarily reflect the views and doctrine of Trilogy Christian Publishing or the Trinity Broadcasting Network.

10 9 8 7 6 5 4 3 2 1
Library of Congress Cataloging-in-Publication Data is available.

ISBN 979-8-89333-807-2
ISBN 979-8-89333-808-9 (ebook)

PREFACE

Growing up, my favorite book to read in the Bible was the book of Proverbs. Despite not having the understanding at the time to fully grasp the meaning of each proverb I read, I did, however, recognize the wisdom that was to be gained by reading and meditating on each proverb. In due time, the truth and wisdom of each proverb would prove to be invaluable in shaping my personal character. A proverb is a short comment that is meant to serve as advice, captures truth, and shows the outcome of being on either side of the good truth.

The inspiration for this book came from real-life practice of the mentioned qualities that were both taught and seen from those who came before me. Early in my life I saw my parents and grandparents struggle and succeed in many ways. It was their character, during all seasons in their life, that built my character. In my life, I have found that the character traits spoken of in this book are the foundation that has helped me in my career and personal achievements, as well as in my service to the church. By the grace and help of the living God, and my desire to serve Him in excellence, although I felt short at times, I was dedicated to practicing the proverbs discussed in this book. Whether it was working full time and attending school full time for ten years straight, becoming a hospital CEO at the age of thirty, founding and starting Word of Christian Church with my family, or starting the Relentless Youth Group, it was practicing these proverbs that propelled me forward to not only experience success, but to experience continuous success. It is my hope that these proverbs will inspire, help, and teach both leaders and future leaders at all stages and in all seasons in their life. If any person practices these proverbs diligently, success is truly within their grasp.

ACKNOWLEDGEMENTS

This book is dedicated first to my impressive mother, Lily Jaso Serrano. My mother for many years worked multiple jobs at the same time and went to school while working full time, owning a business, serving, and helping to start a church from the ground up, all while raising a family. Her integrity, hard work, consistency, character, heart to help people, and motivation were unmatched (I, many times, had a hard time keeping up). I am eternally grateful for not just what she did and demonstrated, but also for her perseverance in all things. Her example never allowed me to give up or say the words "I can't." She is the best person I have ever met in my life. Many others have done great, but for me and to me, she exceeds them all.

Secondly, to the great men of my family who came before me: my dad and both my grandfathers, whom I admire most because of the way others spoke of them and admired them for their hard work and selfless lifestyles. These men showed me by example at a young age that hard work is necessary, rewarded, and required to get ahead. My mother and they did not just tell me to be better; they showed me how to do it. They are the embodiments of the aim this book is conveying. I wish each of them could have read

Proverbs for a Great Leader

this book and that I could tell them how what they showed me has guided me in so many ways. It was their own example and sacrifice that paved the way for me to build on what they demonstrated. Through them, I learned how to be successful in what I set my mind on at a young age. I am confident that in their life wisdom, they knew it would come to pass all along.

To Lee and Lily Serrano, my mom and dad. To my very hard-working brothers, Lee Joseph Serrano, Jr. and Luke Serrano, and to my very hard-working grandfathers, Luis Serrano and Felix Jaso. Thank you for all you did for me, and I hope this book captures each of your values and each of your character traits as I saw and experienced them.

Lastly, to my supportive wife, Annabel Serrano, who has always encouraged and celebrated with me. Her love and support made it easy during the tired and hard times to not only keep going, but to keep a spirit of excellence.

INTRODUCTION

Being smart is just the starting point. Having the minimum qualifications (education, experience, certifications, and licensure) gets you in the door. This book highlights the necessary attributes needed for a leader not just to succeed, but to understand how to succeed continuously. A good leader experiences levels of success, but has a limited ceiling. A great leader will experience continuous success that is without limits, despite the presence of difficult circumstances, difficult people, and personal struggles. Each chapter of this book identifies and teaches a major personal attribute needed to be not just a good leader, but a great one. As you read this book it will change your perspective, it will cause you to look at yourself the hardest (most necessary), and it will serve as a guide to keep you in a state of perpetual victory. The personal attributes learned in this book are useful in any setting, and are required to be successful in any setting.

This book is meant to be a reference that the reader can return to from time to time to remind them of the qualities needed to stay in a state of success.

Leaders are not just those with titles; they are found

Proverbs for a Great Leader

in homes, schools, teams, churches, community organizations, and events. This book, put into practice, will help serve as a guide for those wanting to truly have an impact, no matter the setting.

CHAPTER 1: HUMILITY

"When pride comes, then comes shame; but with the humble is wisdom" (Proverbs 11:2 NKJV).

True humility is a rare character trait but a necessary attribute of a great leader. Humility keeps you on top, and it will help you experience new and continuous success regardless of the circumstances. Humble leaders who stay successful don't let past defeats nor past victories hinder their future success. In all seasons, challenges will always be present. However, no matter what has to be overcome, a humble person will continually improve on self and will work diligently until a solution is found, and/or the dry, rough season passes. They will succeed because they honestly evaluate self and change for the better.

1. The humble reinvent themselves constantly and will achieve great heights. The prideful refuse to change, attempt to get by on titles and past successes, or don't think they need to change. They will deal with the same issues for a lifetime.

Proverbs for a Great Leader

2. A prideful person holds on to their lofty opinion, despite the issues it causes. A humble person examines their own personal motives, thoughts, and actions continuously.

3. A humble person is received and viewed better by others. Pride quickly turns others away.

4. A humble person looks at self the hardest and honestly evaluates the areas that need improvement. This person will take meaningful steps to improve those areas. This is required continuously to be a great leader at all levels of leadership.

5. A humble person learns from failures, whereas a prideful one is quick to blame others.

6. A humble person thoroughly investigates circumstances, problems, and complaints present. A prideful person is quick to become defensive and voice their narrow opinions without any contribution.

7. A humble person considers if there is any wisdom or truth behind the criticism, but is not destroyed by it. A prideful person is offended by it and will miss the lesson, leading to stunted growth. This person is destined to repeat their mistakes, ending only in failure and frustration.

Humility

8. A humble person takes heed when facing barriers and considers them as an opportunity to change, adapt, and improve. The prideful can't see past the barriers and will be limited by them. The only options a prideful person has when barriers are present are to give up, fail, or stay stagnant, because they refuse to look at self and make the necessary changes.

9. The humble person takes advice from many advisors; a prideful person plans his own ways and becomes offended when their plans fail.

10. A humble person takes time to build people up, and an arrogant person is insecure around others who are capable.

11. A humble person's best teachers are setbacks, failures, and discipline. The prideful are quick to give up because of setbacks, failures, and discipline.

12. The humble welcome fair discipline and appropriate correction. Prideful people don't accept correction and become resentful because of it.

13. Opportunities are found most often in chaotic environments that require much cleaning. The humble find opportunities in these places, and they will

achieve what others could not because they are motivated by the opportunity. The prideful will refuse to clean up after others, as they feel shorted or taken advantage of. They miss many opportunities and often can't comprehend why.

14. The humble see the teaching during the struggle; the pride only see the struggle.

15. The humble see problems in an organization as an opportunity to fix, rebuild, and teach. The prideful see and use problems as a deflection of their own issues.

16. The humble master even the smallest of tasks, and the prideful think themselves too big for them.

17. The humble leader goes above and beyond and does not seek recognition, whereas the prideful sound the alarm when extra is asked of them.

18. The humble leader examines bad outcomes as a measure of their actions, oversight, speech, and abilities. A prideful person does not hold themselves accountable for them.

19. When the plans of a humble person fail, they examine them diligently with great care to determine the cause. A prideful person makes excuses and disdains personal accountability.

Humility

20. A humble person requests, whereas a prideful one makes demands, deals in absolutes, and gives ultimatums.

21. The humble admit when they are wrong and avoid self-destruction; the prideful hold on to their ways and opinions, even if destruction is at hand.

22. A humble person learns much and builds character in small beginnings, whereas a prideful person despises small beginnings and feels entitled to unmerited promotion.

23. The humble person puts in the necessary work, knowing success and promotion will come in due season; the arrogant person does enough to get by and wonders why they are passed up.

24. A humble person learns from the good, the bad, and the unfair. A prideful person takes credit for the good, is destroyed during the bad, and complains and quits during the unfair.

25. A humble person respects leadership; an arrogant person will secretly attempt to destroy leadership as they refuse personal accountability.

26. A prideful (arrogant) person is a fault-finder in others and will often deflect accountability from self.

Proverbs for a Great Leader

The humble person works with people, knowing that they have limitations (not ignoring them), in an attempt to help them to overcome.

27. A humble person welcomes wise counselors; a prideful person's heart is hardened to the needed advice.

28. A humble person knows their limitations and seeks those who are strong where they are weak. A prideful person does not know what they do not know. This can only lead to shame when trials reveal their incompetence.

29. The prideful person desires quick success; the humble work hard and diligently until they are ready to be successful, and success finds them.

30. A prideful person desires titles and recognition. The humble work hard for the right reasons and not for recognition. At the right moment, the humble will receive proper honors and recognition that will be meaningful and cherished for a lifetime.

31. The humble leader knows their weaknesses and is not intimidated by them. The prideful will not admit their weaknesses, and this becomes a great danger to themselves, others, and the organization.

Humility

32. A humble person is not defeated by their own mistakes, but will learn and grow from them. The prideful make excuses and often do not change until it brings them to ruin.

33. A humble person listens when emotions are high. This results in peace, truth, and a better outcome. The prideful are quick to argue and defend. This is received as a lack of empathy and compassion, and will only make a bad situation worse.

34. The prideful person uses the word "my" to refer to their area of responsibility. This is a symptom of arrogance that is not perceived well by others.

35. The prideful focus on titles and credentials that feed their ego. The humble let their work speak for itself and quickly earn more respect than the prideful.

36. A humble leader humbly serves first and understands and appreciates the learning that takes place during the serving.

37. The prideful voice their opinions and yet do nothing, whereas the humble work to provide solutions.

38. The humble person takes time to consider all angles of a decision or disagreement. The prideful will

Proverbs for a Great Leader

hold on to their opinion despite the truth in front of them. Their decisions are often to people-please (a louder influence than the truth) their inner circle, despite not being the right thing to do.

CHAPTER 2:
HARD WORK

⚑"The soul of a lazy man desires, and has nothing; but the soul of the diligent shall be made rich" (Proverbs 13:4 NJKV).

If you are afraid of hard work, you can't lead successfully. A great leader leads by example first. Whether good or bad, the work ethic of a leader will be replicated in their environment. A great leader, surrounded by a hard-working team, accomplishes many great things.

1. Hard work is absolutely necessary for the successful person to become successful.

2. The inheritance of the hard worker is promotion, favor, and blessings, and they become a blessing to their employer, family, environment, and community.

3. The successful do not scoff, resent, or fear hard work. They embrace it with eagerness when others don't, and know beforehand that success is found in their work ethic.

Proverbs for a Great Leader

4. The successful leader will not demand hard work from others without first demonstrating it. A leader unwilling or unable to work hard should not be in a position of leadership. It is a matter of time before those unable to demonstrate a hard work ethic will fall short, as well as the organization they are entrusted with.

5. A lazy person is entitled and gets promoted for the wrong reasons. Their success is seasonal and will end only in shame.

6. The hard worker is often resented and disdained at first by those who don't demonstrate the same work ethic. After a short season, they will earn the respect of all.

7. The hard worker will see and seize opportunities which others have missed because of their unwillingness to work for it.

8. The hard worker's work ethic speaks louder than the words of the lazy.

9. The hard worker earns respect and honor that last a lifetime; the slothful only bring failure and then shame.

10. The hard worker is a blessing to their employer

Hard Work

and will receive blessing in the proper season. The slothful weigh down the organization and create a muddy environment that weighs down all.

11. The lazy quickly poison the environment and lower the standards for all. This type of environment quickly becomes a difficult one to change, and failure becomes a strong reality.

12. The lazy attract like-minded people and create a heavy drag on the organization that is not easily moved.

13. The hard worker will do what others won't today, and in due season will go on to achieve what others can't tomorrow.

14. Hard work places a person in position for promotion, where the lazy will remain stagnant and question why they are overlooked.

15. Proper work ethic is learned in youth and is more difficult to adopt the older one becomes.

16. Hard work is learned young and brings rewards at all stages of life.

17. No task is too big or too small for the hard worker. The lazy pawn their work on others and are good at

Proverbs for a Great Leader

avoiding it, despite the consequences.

18. The hard worker will fill in when needed without being asked, because they see the need. The lazy see a problem and voice their opinion about it but are unwilling to be part of the solution.

19. The hard worker earns much; the lazy expect much without doing much.

20. The hard worker will always do what is necessary because it's right in their heart. The lazy become entitled and will feel wronged when extra is asked of them.

21. The lazy make it known to all when they complete a task. The hard worker quietly does their work without expecting gratitude or acknowledgment from others.

22. The hard worker puts in extra effort consistently and is able to complete much. The lazy worker will always do the minimum and yet will always expect much.

23. The hard worker can be trusted with much, and the lazy deserve little, yet expect much.

24. The hard worker is humble, and the lazy are prideful.

Hard Work

25. The lazy put minimum effort and yet broadcast their efforts; the hard worker deserves recognition but will not ask for it because of their humility.

26. The hard worker arrives early and leaves late. They will quickly be promoted, recognized, and rewarded. The lazy expect to be paid for every minute of their time, but not necessarily for their work.

27. The fruits of the hard worker are enjoyed by the next generation.

28. The hard worker knows the benefits of their efforts. Their hard work will be rewarded, and they will experience accomplishments that they will always cherish.

29. The hard worker will often be criticized most by the person who does less.

30. The lazy find ways to avoid real work, while the hard worker springs into action when confronted with challenging tasks.

31. A great leader will weed out the lazy and promote the hard worker to create a strong organization that can't be rivaled.

Proverbs for a Great Leader

32. The ability to work harder than others more than makes up for a disadvantaged starting point.

33. A great leader measures progress and doesn't give up or make excuses if they fall short; rather, they are inspired to work harder. A great leader with self-discipline may fall short but will be inspired to exceed their previous performance.

34. Hard work inspires others.

35. Often there are people who possess knowledge, necessary skills, and training, yet will demonstrate a poor work ethic. These people waste their knowledge, skills, abilities, and training.

36. Hard work is what sets talented people apart from people capable of greatness.

37. Hard work will always produce a harvest.

38. Hard workers produce; the lazy only consume.

CHAPTER 3: CONSISTENCY

"Therefore, my beloved brethren, be steadfast, immovable, always abounding in the work of the Lord, knowing that your labor is not in vain in the Lord" (1 Corinthians 15:58 NKJV).

A great leader must practice consistency. They do not waste an opportunity to work toward their goals. A person who is consistent is a strong person. These are the people needed to create a strong organization.

1. Consistency is necessary to achieve true success.

2. Consistency is done privately first, and is praised publicly later.

3. Successful leaders practice consistency daily.

4. A successful leader stays consistent in their values and efforts.

5. Consistency means daily accountability in working and completing tasks aligned with the goals. A great leader has daily goals, weekly goals, and yearly goals.

Proverbs for a Great Leader

6. Consistency comes from proper motivation that is found in purpose.

7. Consistency in hard work transforms "average" to "great."

8. A good leader must stay consistent through criticism when working to change a bad environment.

9. Consistency is a daily decision and if completed daily, pays great dividends in the future that last a lifetime.

10. A consistent person is a dependable one. A dependable person is a promotable person.

11. A consistent person is a persistent one. A persistent person will create success, promotion, and advancement.

12. A consistent person understands how to keep moving forward during struggles when others are defeated by them.

13. There are many factors that lead to true success. A consistent leader will struggle in their pursuit for success, but will work diligently toward the mark until they are successful. Often the struggle is real and persistent, until one day success manifests, just like the great harvest of the farmer.

Consistency

14. A consistent person does not waste the hours of the day, but makes the most of them.

15. A consistent person advances quickly, leaving others who are unwilling behind. The unwilling person is often unable to comprehend why they remain the same and are not getting promoted.

16. A consistent person's values are ingrained, and they will be bothered when others do not demonstrate similar values.

17. A consistent person sets the bar high. This elevates the other good people around them, but will naturally expose the bad.

18. A consistent person works at being successful and will not be stopped by their mistakes. It is a matter of time before they learn how to be successful.

19. A consistent person acquires much knowledge and is valuable to their organization.

20. A consistent person's success is not based on luck; it is earned. Few will understand how they were able to achieve their success.

21. A consistent person has the direction that will lead to success. They have a plan and work that plan

daily. At any time, they can explain the current progress of the plan.

22. A consistent person will be successful in the future and will reap benefits for a lifetime because they are consistent daily.

23. When a leader is unable to be consistent daily, it is time to step down.

24. A great leader practices consistency continuously, even though results are not yet visible. Because they stay consistent no matter the circumstances, they will not just be a good leader but a great leader.

25. A great leader will have much influence, because they can be trusted to be consistently dependable to accomplish much. This person understands the behaviors and actions that are needed to be effective and efficient. They are diligent in practicing them daily.

26. A consistent person understands the power of training and practice. A great leader will master their training, and in turn will master their performance. These people clearly understand that greatness comes from preparation and determination.

Consistency

27. Once a person understands what behaviors result in success, they must be consistent to demonstrate them habitually.

28. A great leader remains steady and unmoved when criticism surfaces. They will stay consistent in practicing the behaviors that helped them to achieve their greatness in the first place.

29. A consistent person is one whose actions match their speech.

30. A great leader understands that great outcomes come from small but consistent actions.

31. A great leader has a great conviction that if they are not consistently improving, then they are remaining stagnant and are left behind. Those who remain stagnant quickly become irrelevant.

CHAPTER 4: INTEGRITY

"The integrity of the upright will guide them, but the perversity of the unfaithful will destroy them" (Proverbs 11:3 NKJV).

The integrity of a leader will always be tested. In any leadership role there will be challenges, wrongly motivated influences, temptations, and conflict that will test a leader's resolve to the core, revealing whether that leader possesses true integrity. A great leader is great because they display true integrity at all times.

1. A great leader recognizes integrity and will hire those who demonstrate it.

2. Integrity should be the biggest factor when entrusting people with great responsibility. The leader's integrity determines success or failure.

3. Integrity is evident in deeds, and not just by words.

4. A good leader who has integrity is not self-serving, but clearly understands what it means to be a good steward.

Proverbs for a Great Leader

5. Integrity is doing things unnoticed, not to get noticed,

6. A person with integrity searches for the truth in a matter; the untrustworthy conceal the truth and/or deflect away from it.

7. Integrity breeds confidence and trust in others.

8. A person's true integrity brings the best defense when wrongfully accused.

9. A person with integrity does not let known problems fester, but can always be trusted to address them.

10. A person with integrity is not prideful, but takes pride in their work.

11. A person with integrity is governed by their morals and character.

12. A person with integrity can be trusted to make the right decisions, despite how difficult they may be. This is a person who can be trusted with much.

13. Integrity is a proper guide during a trial.

14. Integrity means being fair with all, not being accepted by all.

Integrity

15. A person's integrity is shown most when tested.

16. The integrity of a person is a louder influence than the wrongful influence of the wrong people.

17. A person with integrity knows when to speak and when not to. They are not a person who voices their opinion for all to hear in an effort to seek validation from others.

18. A person with integrity is one who admits their mistakes and shortcomings freely. This person can be trusted with great responsibility.

19. Trust flows from integrity.

20. Integrity is not displayed by well-spoken words but becomes evident through deeds, decisions, and behaviors, and will always manifest when tough situations manifest.

21. Integrity is not seasonal or based on circumstance; rather, it's persistent and consistent and demonstrated for a lifetime.

22. A person with integrity will diligently review details to avoid mistakes and misunderstandings.

23. A person with integrity does not waste the precious time and resources of the organization.

Proverbs for a Great Leader

24. A person who has true integrity provides sound reasoning for their decisions. A bad leader often makes decisions that derive from a place of pride and/or wrongfully-motivated influences. A great leader will stand when their decisions circle back to them, and a bad leader will be exposed or destroyed by the decisions they make.

25. A person with integrity will always demonstrate a character that has great regard for the quality of their work and the work of those around them. This person is a promotable person.

26. A person with true integrity is not easily influenced and will properly research matters to determine their viewpoint or position. A bad leader or bad employee easily believes gossip, without first searching for the truth in a matter before they form their opinion. These people will voice their opinion loudly for all to hear, even if it hurts good people, despite it being true or false.

27. A person with true integrity is easily noticed. These people, when given opportunity or during their pursuits, will make mistakes but will be honest about them and not be defeated by them. These are the people who have the potential for so much more.

Integrity

28. A person with true integrity demonstrates passion, organization, hard work, and excellent interpersonal skills. A great leader searches for these qualities when looking for future leaders to promote.

29. A person desiring to advance who has true integrity will search for a good organization to work hard for, and will also not step on others to get to the desired position.

30. Integrity is the key to fair business dealings.

31. A great leader who has integrity searches for the truth during times of conflict and learns how to tame emotions, both in self and in others.

32. A person with integrity takes ownership, and sees problems as their personal problem to work on until they are fixed. A person without integrity will see problems and do nothing, because they believe it is someone else's responsibility. They refuse to take ownership or to demonstrate personal accountability.

33. A person with integrity will not provide an opinion without first researching the facts. Those who lack integrity carelessly speak their minds with no regard for the truth, nor the negative impacts their words may have.

CHAPTER 5: STAYING MOTIVATED

"And let us not grow weary while doing good, for in due season we shall reap if we do not lose heart" (Galatians 6:9 NKJV).

Staying motivated is necessary to becoming a great leader. A great leader must stay motivated in the tough times, lonely times, confusing times, scary times, and lastly, in the good times. A person who stays motivated will experience true success. It is not a matter of "if," but rather just a matter of time.

1. A great leader will stay motivated by the good that can be done, despite the bad.

2. A great leader will not be moved by the bad but will remain motivated, because they know what is to be gained when the bad turns to good.

3. Staying motivated is an equal part of success, as much as skills and abilities. Capable people often lose heart and will fall short of success, because they do not stay motivated.

Proverbs for a Great Leader

4. A motivated person understands that success takes time and is a process.

5. True motivation comes from a keen sense of purpose.

6. A motivated person will out-work and will outlast others.

7. Motivation comes mostly from being valued. This creates a clear understanding of purpose. Valued employees give more.

8. A motivated person improves the environment through the energy they bring. This energy is felt by others and will inspire others to do the same. An unmotivated person creates a heavy drag that is also felt by others.

9. Motivated people do not give up until they are successful. They will find the path around obstacles or will find a way to move them.

10. Motivated people know what it takes to be great and are not afraid to carry it out.

11. Motivated people do not scoff at a challenge, but are driven by it.

12. Motivated people know the benchmarks and will strive to surpass them.

Staying Motivated

13. Motivation is the spark to the engine; purpose is the fuel to the engine. Only when these are combined does the capacity to move forward with great momentum happen.

14. Motivated people know the path (plan), work the plan, and hold themselves accountable to the plan daily. This means they work toward their goals daily. This person looks back on their life and has much to show for it. The unmotivated stay the same, deal with the same issues, and have the same reasons for not moving forward year by year.

15. Motivated individuals require little supervision and will display great initiative. These people will seek to learn their assigned tasks with great diligence until they master it. Once mastered, they are ready for promotion.

16. Motivated people are not defeated by setbacks, negative individuals, or tough situations. On the contrary, they are motivated to demonstrate what can be.

17. Motivated people know the process and quickly communicate where they are in the process.

18. Motivated people do not give up during the process.

Proverbs for a Great Leader

19. A truly motivated leader does not require outside validation to stay motivated, but is motivated by their strong character from within.

20. A great leader knows how to stay motivated despite the validation of others. A bad leader is broken without validation by others. An aspiring leader must learn that validation takes time, and often will not come until they have overcome criticism first.

21. A truly motivated person always stands out and is easily recognizable. These are the people that much can be built around.

22. To stay motivated, one must realize that criticism will always be close at hand. No great leader ever went without it.

23. Motivated people genuinely care.

24. A motivated person will be a blessed person in many ways.

25. Motivated people will lift others up by their example in a way that gives permission for others to follow.

26. Motivation is contagious and gives hope and inspiration to others.

Staying Motivated

27. A motivated person must learn to stay positive when others are not. Many times, people will attempt to project their negative views, inabilities, and limitations on others. Great leaders do not let negative environments negatively affect them; rather, they have the capability to transform their environment for the better.

28. A motivated person has the conviction to pick themselves up, dust themselves off, and move forward relentlessly until they succeed.

29. A motivated person will learn what it takes and then go out and do it. Many people talk, but the motivated person does.

30. A great leader must get organized, evaluate, and outline what the path to success will be. Once done, then they must have the motivation to move forward with great intensity, without stopping until success is realized.

31. In pursuit of success, a great leader will not lean on or be defeated by excuses or challenges. They demonstrate the necessary motivation to work past them. Great leaders do not ignore that challenges exist, but they stay motivated until they learn how to overcome them.

CHAPTER 6: PERSPECTIVE

"Do not be deceived: 'Evil company corrupts good habits'" (1 Corinthians 15:33 NKJV).

Having the right perspective keeps a leader focused and motivated. A person's perspective can be easily influenced. It's imperative that a great leader evaluate their perspective frequently, because it will ultimately guide how they act, respond, and make their decisions. It is most certain for any leader of any kind and an absolute fact that they will face constant criticism. It is necessary for a great leader to know how to manage and handle criticism.

1. A person's perspective influences all their decisions and how they treat others.

2. The best perspective comes from a big circle of influence and not a small one. The reality of a small circle is seen in parts, but not the whole. People who make opinions and decisions based on their small circles of influence will often be led down a bad path that ends only in disappointment and shame.

Proverbs for a Great Leader

3. The proper perspective of a good leader is vision-focused. They know their vision and push towards it constantly. The wrong perspective is one that is led by fear and only breeds negativity towards a better future.

4. A great leader's perspective comes from a keen sense of good core values. A bad leaders' biggest motivation is self-gain. This becomes the biggest driver of their perspective and ultimately their decision making.

5. A great leader works to understand the perspective of others that brings better insight and builds a better organization. A bad leader holds on their views, even to their self-destruction.

6. A great leader's perspective is moldable within the confines of their core beliefs.

7. A great leader's perspective often comes from experiences, but it is never limited by past achievements nor past defeats.

8. The perspective of a great leader is driven by service and stewardship. A bad leader's perspective is self-serving, self-gain, and arrogance.

Perspective

9. The great perspective of a great leader stays unchanged in the midst of difficulties because of their strong character. The bad perspective of a bad leader is easily noticed and is one of resentment, blame, anger, and self-doubt.

10. Obtaining a proper perspective is a sign of great wisdom.

11. Proper perspective is the beginning point necessary to start the improvement process.

12. Proper perspective is obtained from sincere listening and from one who seeks the truth and diligently examines the details.

13. The pure perspective of a great leader is not moved by the negative perception of others.

14. Perspective, when properly attuned, provides the necessary insight to building a proper plan.

15. The proper perspective of a great leader is to take ownership of the organization and is evident through their work ethic, energy, and willingness to empower others, and will always be goal-oriented. The perspective of a bad leader is motivated by self-promotion and is evident when they blame, complain, and take great offense if not agreed with.

Proverbs for a Great Leader

16. Having proper perspective is knowing how the fix needs to happen and the fruit it will yield. This in turn brings the necessary conviction to stay steady and unmoved during the criticism that is sure to come during the fixing stage.

17. A great leader who has proper perspective will not let the perception of others dictate their behaviors.

18. In order to gain proper perspective, a good leader must have the humility to examine self first.

19. To gain proper perspective, a good leader must be willing to consider all the facts and not just the limited opinions of others.

20. Once obtained, proper perspective is the motivating force that helps a great leader push through any challenge.

21. Perspective changes with age and experience. A great leader changes, molds, and adapts for the better. A bad leader holds on to flawed thinking that will lead to frustration and missed opportunities.

22. When challenged, or in the face of a struggle, a proper perspective is blurred at first. A great leader knows how to slow the situation down until the best plan and response can be developed.

Perspective

23. A properly developed perspective helps a leader in their decision making. A great leader who demonstrates proper perspective is recognizable by how efficiently the leader makes decisions and the quality of their decisions.

24. Knowledge, practice, character, and environment all shape perspective. A great leader will not let a negative environment influence their perspective, but rather will work hard to change the negative perception of that environment.

25. All great leaders who have accomplished what others thought impossible knew that their vision was possible first. These individuals had to remain determined to stay the course despite constant criticism, temporary setbacks, having to create that which did not yet exist, and real obstacles. The conviction to stay the course came from a proper perspective.

26. A great leader is not one who is simply able to see the issues, but rather displays the courage and wisdom to overcome them. A bad leader thinks highly of themselves because they can see the issues and simply voice their opinion about it.

Proverbs for a Great Leader

27. A great leader has the wisdom and understanding to know that they will always face criticism. The more successful they are, the more criticism will be a close companion. The proper perspective to overcome it is to face it head on with dignity, integrity, and professionalism.

28. To obtain a proper perspective to lead an organization, a great leader must have a good sense of where the organization is headed. This comes from honestly evaluating where the organization has been, what present market challenges exist, where the organization needs to be to be successful in the future, and what is the vision needed to rally all those involved. This is the foundation for building a proper plan.

29. A great leader can always communicate, with great conviction, the reasoning behind each decision they make. This comes from having a proper perspective.

30. No person is owed anything. The successful person has this perspective and will not be hindered by it. The perspective of the defeated is entitlement. Entitlement only ends in shame.

CHAPTER 7: SELF-DISCIPLINE

"For the moment all discipline seems painful rather than pleasant, but later it yields the peaceful fruit of righteousness to those who have been trained by it" (Hebrews 12:11 ESV).

Self-discipline is holding oneself accountable consistently. A person who does not demonstrate self-discipline is not fit for leadership nor is to be entrusted with great responsibility. A self-disciplined individual is self-motivated, consistently shows initiative, and is willing to make the necessary sacrifices to do what is needed to get ahead (extra studying, extra sets in a workout, arriving to work early, etc.).

1. A self-disciplined individual is not controlled or influenced by emotions and negative influences. They pursue what they know is right despite them.

2. A great leader is one who understands that self-discipline is to do what is necessary to become an expert in their craft.

Proverbs for a Great Leader

3. Self-discipline is necessary to be a great leader. This quality must be developed before promotion happens, and is also why promotion happens.

4. The opportunity to practice self-discipline is available with each new day. A successful person takes advantage of each new opportunity, and the unsuccessful waste much opportunity.

5. A self-disciplined person works hard to build their understanding.

6. A self-disciplined individual is an organized one. This person can manage much and will accomplish much.

7. A self-disciplined individual understands that strength is built through struggles. They look at self and find ways to improve most during the struggle and are not defeated by them, because they are determined to rise above them.

8. A self-disciplined individual knows the qualities that are needed to be successful and practices them daily.

9. Self-discipline is looking at self to examine for weaknesses. One who is truthful in this is the one who will not have limits on what they can achieve.

Self-Discipline

10. A great leader understands that self-discipline involves holding oneself accountable to the qualities and behaviors that they demand from others.

11. Self-discipline starts early in the day. A great leader is the one who wakes early in the day to make the most of each waking hour.

12. True self-discipline considers the details.

13. A truly self-disciplined individual does not wait on others to ask or to be invited to get involved. They show initiative and will demonstrate the wisdom to know when and where to step in and take action.

14. A self-disciplined individual will not put off tasks until tomorrow when there is room in the day to fit in more.

15. A good leader who is self-disciplined is well organized with their to-do list and works hard on that list daily.

16. The self-discipline to consistently do extra is ingrained in the great leader. A bad leader attempts to get by on doing the bare minimum.

17. Consistent self-discipline is rewarded in all aspects of life, including professionally and personally.

Proverbs for a Great Leader

18. A self-disciplined individual requires minimal supervision. These people are fit for leadership and can manage much responsibility.

19. A self-disciplined individual is consistent in making good choices. These people have the ability to make tough choices, even when they know it will create inconveniences that others are not willing to endure.

20. Self-discipline is knowing and demonstrating the necessary behaviors to achieve great goals.

21. Self-discipline is knowing what must be sacrificed to achieve the goal. Sacrifice is always necessary for any true achievement.

22. Self-disciplined individuals are always goal-oriented. Completing a task and seeing the fruits of their labor bring a satisfaction that builds their spirit.

23. A self-disciplined individual will not ignore problems, but will also display the wisdom and tact to know when to properly address issues and when not to address them emotionally.

24. A self-disciplined individual who understands balance will make the most of each moment by learn-

Self-Discipline

ing how to always be present and not absent-minded. This is a difficult skill to master, but great leaders will excel at this.

25. A self-disciplined individual reflects on each day and week to see where they fall short and what areas they must pursue the next day. The person who does this will become great and will look back on the conclusion of each week with great satisfaction at a job well done.

26. A self-disciplined individual recognizes distractions and knows that they are the biggest dream-killers.

27. A great leader has the self-discipline to react professionally and cautiously when emotions are running high.

28. A self-disciplined individual knows how to balance great responsibility and is skilled at layering tasks to maximize output with great efficiency.

29. A self-disciplined individual knows what they do not know and is humble enough to know their limits, but also is determined to not be limited by them.

30. Conflict is often the result of competing perspectives. A great leader possesses the self-discipline to

Proverbs for a Great Leader

work at understanding each perspective to develop the best response.

CHAPTER 8:
THE RIGHT PEOPLE

"Two are better than one, because they have a good reward for their labor. For if they fall, one will lift up his companion. But woe to him who is alone when he falls, for he has no one to help him up. Again, if two lie down together, they will keep warm; but how can one be warm alone? Though one may be overpowered by another, two can withstand him. And a threefold cord is not quickly broken" (Ecclesiastes 4:9-12 NKJV).

The Greeks invented the phalanx formation. Properly performed, with the right people performing as a team and a single unit, the phalanx could not be stopped. Each person doing their assigned job correctly was necessary for the phalanx to survive the barrage of attacks and remain unpenetrated. The phalanx gave the ability for a small group to rival a large army. The same is true of any organization. Finding the right people is challenging and takes time, but once done, a great leader is empowered to accomplish so much more. A great leader knows how to turn individuals into a team that works together and not against each other.

Proverbs for a Great Leader

1. A good leader finds success with the right people.

2. A spoiled person spoils the environment, and a spoiled environment has no momentum.

3. The diligent employee is a blessing to their employer; a lazy one weighs them down.

4. The right people bring value and benefits. The wrong people bring more problems than value.

5. A great organization filled with great people is one that thrives. An organization filled with bad people is one that will struggle and have limitations. Tough times reveal what type of people the organization is filled with.

6. A successful leader surrounds themselves with people who are mission-focused and not self-serving.

7. A successful leader recognizes the strength and potential in others and helps them work past their weaknesses.

8. A successful leader is aware of their weaknesses and finds others who excel in areas in which they are weak.

9. In the search for the right people, a good leader will at first be criticized, then later be exalted.

The Right People

10. The right people make a good leader great.

11. Once a culture of excellence is established, the wrong people will no longer fit in. These people depart on their own.

12. A good culture attracts good people; a bad culture attracts bad ones.

13. A great leader evaluates each person fairly, honestly, and with ambitious standards. This is welcomed by the right people and disdained by the wrong.

14. Good people bring energy to the organization, whereas the bad bring only problems.

15. Good people are honest about actual issues but will also work to find solutions. The bad focus on the issues and will use them as reasons not to be motivated.

16. A great leader recognizes good character quickly, and good character is more valuable than good credentials.

17. Good people manage themselves, whereas bad people waste much of the organization's valuable time, effort, and energy.

Proverbs for a Great Leader

18. Good people create value for the organization, and bad create a black hole that consumes everything they touch.

19. The good employees welcome meaningful feedback, whereas the bad become offended by it.

20. A good person lights the room up with their presence that is felt, whereas the bad bring an instant weight. All feel their heaviness.

21. A good person admits mistakes and issues; the bad will attempt to cover them up and hope they are not discovered.

22. A good environment is built with good people and will empower a great leader to stay focused on growth and strategy. A bad environment weighs down the leader with operational issues and forces the leader to delay and even abandon the important functions of a great leader.

23. A good organization with good people will always outshine and outperform the bad one filled with the wrong people.

24. A good hire is worth much; a bad hire costs much.

25. A good organization with good people is not easily built, but is done with patience and consistency. Bad organizations are difficult to overcome.

The Right People

26. A good leader must hold all accountable fairly, honestly, and consistently.

27. A good leader looks good with the right people. The wrong people make a good leader look bad. A path to becoming a great leader is the leader's ability to identify the right people.

28. A great leader builds a great culture with good values. Those who do not represent the same values stand out and become easily noticed.

29. A wise leader empowers others; a bad leader withholds knowledge because of personal insecurities.

30. The effectiveness of a great leader is determined by the leader's ability to assemble the right people. To do so takes time, good judge of character, patience, and persistence.

31. A great leader stays motivated by great people around them. In contrast, a bad leader will struggle most because of the negative views and influence of the bad.

32. A person unfit for leadership often doesn't know what they don't know. This is a great danger to the organization that is not easily overcome. This person's failure will surely come. A person as-

Proverbs for a Great Leader

piring to be a great leader will honestly evaluate their weaknesses, know their limitations, surround themselves with good counsel, and will be diligent in their pursuit to increase in wisdom.

33. Hire good people and succeed. Hire bad people and fail.

34. A great leader who achieves a level of success will reach down and pick others up along the way, to help them reach greater heights.

35. The right people are the strength of an organization and bring strength to the leader.

36. An organization with a few good people can accomplish much. An organization filled with many good people will achieve great inertia that will go on to accomplish so much more.

37. A great leader recognizes that diversity brings value, and that people of various skills and backgrounds are an asset, as they will have a great combined perspective. This is the starting point, but despite that, the leader must achieve unity of purpose, whereby each is working to a common goal and/or vision.

CHAPTER 9: POWER OF INSPIRATION

"We who are strong ought to bear with the failings of the weak and not to please ourselves. Each of us should please our neighbors for their good, to build them up" (Romans 15:1-2 NIV).

Learning to inspire others is a great skill of a great leader. Often leaders are chosen and thrust into leadership by their ability to inspire. An inspired workforce is one that works hard and cohesively and is one that will achieve great outcomes.

1. A successful leader is successful at inspiring others. If you can inspire, you can lead.

2. A great leader inspires people to achieve more than they think is possible.

3. A great leader is honest about the issues, but is able to inspire themselves and others to push through and rise above them.

Proverbs for a Great Leader

4. An inspired individual accomplishes much.

5. An inspired staff achieves great feats.

6. Many people work hard, and many people are smart; few have the ability to inspire.

7. An inspired individual is an energetic individual who breathes life into an environment and organization.

8. Inspiration flows from a source that is pure.

9. A great leader inspires others to hope for better.

10. People follow the person who has the ability to inspire others.

11. Inspiration is the axle that propels the organization forward.

12. A wise leader can see the potential in others and is able to inspire them to work through their weaknesses.

13. An inspired individual creates much; an uninspired person becomes a hindrance that consumes much without creating much.

14. An inspired individual springs into action when a problem surfaces. The uninspired complain, vent,

Power of Inspiration

and do not possess the energy to work through the problems.

15. A successful leader inspires others to want more.

16. A successful leader is capable of inspiring others to change their negative views by getting them to believe that better is possible.

17. Inspiration is the stimulant of hard work.

18. A successful leader inspires others by being energetic, demonstrating a proper grasp of the challenge, plainly articulating a plan, demonstrating compassion, and providing clear solutions needed to overcome.

19. An inspired individual is not overcome or defeated by battles lost; rather, they view them as their best teacher.

20. The presence of a truly inspired individual is easily recognized and felt because of their energy.

21. A great leader inspires others by listening intently first, and being slow to speak second. This shows compassion and sincerity that is the foundation for building trust. Trust is paramount in being able to inspire others.

Proverbs for a Great Leader

22. An inspiring speech is not one with fancy words but is sincere, heartfelt, clearly communicated, and easy to understand. The bad speech of a bad leader deflects, uses fancy words to confuse, and plays down what the actual issues are.

23. Inspiration requires energy, empathy, integrity, passion, and confidence, and demonstrates a keen awareness of social factors.

24. A great leader is one who can handle conflict well. All conflict presents an opportunity to improve and inspire all parties involved, if managed properly.

25. A great leader knows how to stay inspired by having a good grasp of why they do what they do, reflecting the on the profoundly important impacts achieved, identifying and measuring progress, surrounding themselves with good people, and understanding the value of service to others.

26. A truly inspired individual operates at an elevated level. The key to being a great leader is finding and inspiring people to follow the strong example set.

27. An inspired person can overcome much. These people, because they have a sense of purpose, push through fatigue, are not discouraged by naysayers,

Power of Inspiration

stay steady and consistent without yet seeing results, and face challenge after challenge with great determination. This is how winning is done.

CHAPTER 10: OVERCOMING THE STRUGGLE

⸆"And not only that, but we also glory in tribulations, knowing that tribulation produces perseverance; and perseverance, character; and character, hope" (Romans 5:3-4 NKJV).

Nothing great in life comes before struggles and sacrifices. Struggles are guaranteed for all leaders in any type of organization. Learning to overcome difficulties and struggles is what makes a great leader great. It builds the needed confidence, composure, grit, and understanding needed to overcome even bigger obstacles. Winning in life is simply done by the person who can keep moving forward despite the presence of difficulties, setbacks, struggles, and obstacles.

1. Learning to overcome struggles makes a great leader great.

2. Struggles are guaranteed. The measure of a great leader is not how much they struggle; it is how much they can endure those struggles and keep moving forward without giving up.

Proverbs for a Great Leader

3. Many leaders will be limited by their struggles. Great leaders are ones who learn and persist past any struggle to go on to thrive.

4. A great leader sees the vision on the other side of the struggle, whereas a poor leader only focuses on the struggle.

5. Struggles produce character, skills, and great wisdom.

6. Times without struggles produce comfort. Comfortable people tend to grow slowly, or not at all.

7. Struggles force leaders to the greatest learning that takes place out of necessity. That learning will benefit a great leader throughout their lifetime.

8. Motivation and willpower are necessary during the struggle. This comes from purpose.

9. A great leader does not fail when they experience a struggle or setback. They simply have the attitude of learning how not to do something.

10. Showing up and not giving up is half the battle during a struggle.

11. A great team with the right leaders is the biggest asset during the struggles. Many times, the answer

Overcoming the Struggle

to overcome the struggle lies with the group, and not the individual.

12. A great leader will always look back at a struggle to determine if any action could have been taken to prevent the struggle. Even when the issues were created by others.

13. Struggles reveal the weakness in an individual and in an organization. Great leaders use those struggles to shape themselves and the organization. Bad leaders are defeated by them because they lack the humility, discipline, and motivation required to make it through.

14. The future leader who takes the initiative and is doing things is the one who often struggles the most. The leader who is not struggling is ignoring issues and often is the one not doing anything meaningful. These people are complacent. Complacent people do not have a desire to change and will quickly be left behind and become irrelevant in skill, knowledge, and capabilities.

15. Struggles will not end in defeat if the great leader is unwilling to give up.

Proverbs for a Great Leader

16. The ability to navigate struggles will make or break a leader. Often, a great leader does not realize their capabilities until they are forced to navigate the struggle. Additionally, a bad leader will not come to terms with their inabilities until they are revealed by the struggle.

17. All great leaders will face struggles. A great leader will rise to the occasion and be valued and appreciated by their handling of the struggles. A bad leader will be illuminated and will be defeated by their inability to navigate the struggle. Their failure will be swift and seen by all.

18. A great leader springs to action and works hard and extra during the struggles. A bad leader can only do the bare minimum, and as a direct result will be overcome during the times of struggle.

19. Struggles will push the limits of any organization. An organization with the right people has much higher limits that can withstand so much more.

20. Struggles force innovation that otherwise would not have taken place in the absence of the struggle.

21. In such a way that a weightlifter must struggle to the point of failure for the greatest muscle growth,

Overcoming the Struggle

a leader must struggle to develop the characteristics of a genuinely great leader. A leader unwilling to struggle and fail is one who is unfit for leadership.

22. Every victory comes with struggles first. Pushing past the struggles is necessary to get to the place of victory.

23. During the struggle, answers and solutions are unclear and become like a fog. A great leader knows how to stay committed to the vision and will not falter in the vision during the fog. They remain committed to moving forward until the answer comes (a matter of time).

24. Struggles create opportunities to build back better. Great leaders know this and take advantage of each of those opportunities.

25. Struggles reveal the need for change. People are more willing to change when presented with struggles and difficulties.

26. A leader will often feel that they are struggling the most right before a breakthrough happens. A great leader recognizes this and will not be defeated or give up right before the blessing.

Proverbs for a Great Leader

27. Struggles are temporary. But the lessons learned last a lifetime.

28. Struggles, effectively managed, have the ability to bring people closer together.

29. Struggles have a way of uniting people to achieve great tasks.

30. Many great achievements, innovations, and inventions came from motivated people who persisted in struggles.

31. Just like the first flight of an eagle, a person does not fully realize what they can accomplish until struggles force them to action.

32. Overcoming struggles produces confidence, knowledge, and strong character.

33. A young person unwilling to struggle treads water but has no movement. Struggles are a part of life. When they decide to face them head on, they will then learn how success happens. The younger they do this, the more success they will experience.

34. All great leaders were elevated to greatness as a direct result of how they overcame tough struggles.

Overcoming the Struggle

35. Patience, persistence, and endurance are needed when the answers are unclear during a struggle. A great leader has the wisdom to know that answers and solutions will come in time. While they are waiting, investigating, and researching, they have mastered the ability to control their emotions and decisions until then.

36. All leaders will struggle. Struggles will have the effect of separating the bad from the great.

www.ingramcontent.com/pod-product-compliance
Lightning Source LLC
Chambersburg PA
CBHW071532210125
20608CB00046B/1077